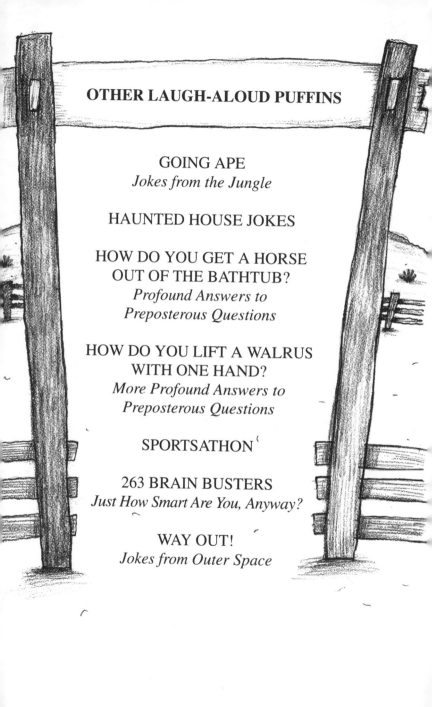

# OTHER LAUGH-ALOUD PUFFINS

# Westward Ho Ho Ho!

## Jokes from the Wild West

### By Victoria Hartman
### Illustrated by G. Brian Karas

PUFFIN BOOKS

# For Michael
## —V.H.

PUFFIN BOOKS
Published by the Penguin Group
Penguin Books USA Inc., 375 Hudson Street, New York, New York 10014, U.S.A.
Penguin Books Ltd, 27 Wrights Lane, London W8 5TZ, England
Penguin Books Australia Ltd, Ringwood, Victoria, Australia
Penguin Books Canada Ltd, 10 Alcorn Avenue, Toronto, Ontario, Canada M4V 3B2
Penguin Books (N.Z.) Ltd, 182–190 Wairau Road, Auckland 10, New Zealand

Penguin Books Ltd, Registered Offices: Harmondsworth, Middlesex, England

First published in the United States of America by Viking Penguin,
a division of Penguin Books USA Inc., 1992
Published in Puffin Books, 1994

1  3  5  7  9  10  8  6  4  2

THE LIBRARY OF CONGRESS HAS CATALOGED THE VIKING PENGUIN EDITION AS FOLLOWS:
Hartman, Victoria. Westward ho ho ho! / Victoria Hartman;
illustrated by G. Brian Karas.    p.    cm.
Summary: A collection of western jokes, riddles, and knock-knocks.
ISBN 0-670-84040-8
1. Wit and humor, Juvenile. 2. West (U.S.)—Juvenile humor  [1. West
(U.S.) Wit and humor. 2. Jokes.]  I. Karas, G. Brian, ill.  II. Title.
PN6163.H35    1992    818'.5402—dc20    91-29849    CIP    AC

Puffin Books ISBN 0-14-036851-5
Printed in the United States of America
Set in Optima

# Contents

# Chapter One
# Roaming the Range

*Knock, knock.*
*Who's there?*
*Mustang.*
*Mustang who?*
> Mustang up the laundry.

KING: How did the princess track down her mate?
QUEEN: She followed the hoof prince.
KING: Where did she see him?
QUEEN: On the bridal path.

*Knock, knock.*
*Who's there?*
*Cadillac.*
*Cadillac who?*
> Cadillac a warm barn at the end of the day.

*Knock, knock.*
*Who's there?*
*Lassoing.*
*Lassoing who?*
>*Lassoing money will have to pay it back.*

MIKE: What has more than one tongue and goes
>*crackle, crackle?*

VIC: How about a two-headed witch?
MIKE: Good try. Guess again.
VIC: I don't know. What does have more than one
>tongue and goes *crackle, crackle?*

MIKE: A campfire.

*Knock, knock.*
*Who's there?*
*Illegal.*
*Illegal who?*
>*Illegal needs some medicine quick.*

*Knock, knock.*
*Who's there?*
*Baaa.*
*Baaa who?*
> Baaa bells help sheep develop biceps.

*What kind of spider makes a lot of noise when it's sleeping?*
> A snore-pion.

*What was the gladiator doing out West?*
> He was a-Roman on the range.

JIM: Cowboys sure do work hard. How do they get paid?
RANCHER: Oh, they get paid with buffalo bills.

*Why did the bear leave his umbrella at home?*
    He was a drizzly bear.


Cowboy Nick: How do you find out which horses like
    to run?
Rancher Rick: I take a gallop poll.


*What kind of dinosaur do you find at a rodeo?*
    A bronco-saurus.


*Why did the rattlers have a reunion?*
    It was for old times' snake.

*What do you call a clothing thief on the run?*
    A dress-perado.


*Why did the rainbow go out West?*
    It wanted to see the Old Prism Trail.

*Why did the game-show host go out West?*
        He wanted to see the Old Quizzem Trail.

*Why did Tonto think he was seeing double?*
        Because of the Clone Ranger.

A lawman, by name Wyatt Earp,
Went wild if you called him a twerp;
    He'd fake a deep slumber
    Then eat a cucumber
And blow you away with a burp.

# Chapter Two
# Chuck Wagon

*Knock, knock.*
*Who's there?*
*Horsing around.*
*Horsing around who?*
> Horsing around the campfire if someone
> plays the guitar.

*What did the wild-West chicken call her gun-toting*
*daughter?*
> Annie Yolkly.

*How does the cavalry make soup?*
> With stock-ade.

*What's the difference between a jalapeño and a cold spy?*
> One's a chili pepper, the other's a chilly peeper.

TEX: Say, that chuck-wagon chef is shaking with fright.
HANK: Did he see a mountain lion?
TEX: Could be. I betcha he serves us some panicakes.
HANK: That's silly. Panicakes indeed!
TEX: Oh, well then. Griddlequakes.
HANK: Oooh. How waffle.

*Knock, knock.*
*Who's there?*
*Texas.*
*Texas who?*
Texas five minutes to heat a can of beans.

*Why did the monsters go out West for dinner?*
They were invited to a blob-ecue.

*What kind of pepper makes you scream?*
Holler-peño peppers.

*What are the favorite peppers in Hawaii?*
Hula-peño peppers.

*What's a duck's favorite party dip?*
Quackamolé.

*Why did the corn chips gossip?*
They had a lot to taco about.

*What kind of corn chips can you count on?*
Notch-o's.

SARA: Why did the hungry bank robber put his money in a pickle barrel?

DANNY: I don't know. Sounds like he wasn't using his brine.

SARA: What a wise guy!

DANNY: Okay, why *did* the hungry bank robber put his money in a pickle barrel?

SARA: He wanted some sourdough bread.

*Knock, knock.*
*Who's there?*
*Beans.*
*Beans who?*
Beans so long since I had a good hotdog.

*What is an insect's favorite Tex-Mex food?*
Ant-chiladas.

*What is the coldest vegetable?*
    A chilly pepper.

*Why was the cowboy interested in the frying pan?*
    He had a steak in it.

*What kind of meat do you dust the floor with?*
    Sweep steaks.

*How do sheep like their beef?*
    Baa-baa-cued.

*What do Texans eat when they're in Ireland?*
    Chili con blarney.

*How do Texans like their pie?*
    Pie a'lamo.

*Why did the cowboys stop at Carvel?*
It was custard's last stand.

*How do Texas hairdressers like their beef?*
Barber-cued.

*Who brought tropical fruit to the wild West?*
The papaya-neers.

*What vegetable do steer ropers like?*
Bronco-li.

*What kind of candy do the bad guys like?*
Var-mints.

What do cowgirls put on their pancakes?
Maple stirrup.

A chuck-wagon cook named Corinne
Cooked stew which kept everyone thin;
    To a big pot of rice
    She'd add two or three mice
Plus a boot and some rattlesnake skin.

*Knock, knock.*
*Who's there?*
*Sheriff.*
*Sheriff who?*
       Sheriff there's enough candy to go around.

*Knock, knock.*
*Who's there?*
*Carmen.*
*Carmen who?*
       Carmen get it!

# Chapter Three
# Wide Open Spaces

*What do you call a bison that gets tired while running?*
    A huff and puffalo.

*How did the pioneers cry?*
    With front tears.

AMY: What swimming style do they do out West?
JANET: The crawl of the wild.

VULTURE #1: Why haven't you answered the door?
VULTURE #2: I didn't hear the buzzard.
VULTURE #1: I think it's your date. Where are you
      going?
VULTURE #2: To a concert.
VULTURE #1: Where?
VULTURE #2: At the vultural center.

*Why do people make so many phone calls to California?*
        It's the dialed, dialed West.

*How does a snake refuse an offer?*
        It says, "No fang you."

*Why did the sailor get on the prairie schooner?*
        He wanted some great plains sailing.

*What do a harmonica and a boxer have in common?*
        They both receive blows.

*What holds up a stagecoach?*
        Wheels.

*What do the air force and the prairie have in common?*

They both have planes (plains).

*Knock, knock.*
*Who's there?*
*Lion cubs.*
*Lion cubs who?*

Lion cubs don't tell the truth.

BUFFALO BOB: Do you see those sleeping cattle over there?

BUFFALO BILL: Yes, I do, but I thought they were bull-dozers.

*What do brides wear at a pioneer wedding?*

A wagon train.

*Knock, knock.*
*Who's there?*
*Antelope.*
*Antelope who?*
> Antelope with uncle last week.

*What birds stick together?*
> Vel-crows.

*Knock, knock.*
*Who's there?*
*Bison.*
*Bison who?*
> Bison, see you next week.

A teacher by name of Miss Whacktus
Fell from her horse on a cactus;
   "Durn," she'd opine
   As she pulled out each spine,
"I'm sorely in need of more practice."

*Why did Rover get friendly with the covered wagon?*
        It was a waggin' train.

*Why couldn't the bakers in the wild West hear
so well?*
        They had pie in ears.

*How do prairie schooners hear?*
        With wagon ears.

*What did they call magic in frontier days?*
    Westward ho-cus pocus.

*Why did the ghosts go out West?*
    They were pioneering spirits.

ED: What's the difference between an ear of corn with
        no kernels and a baby grizzly?
JOHN: I can't imagine, but I wouldn't want to bite into
        either. Please inform me.
ED: An ear of corn without kernels is a bare cob. A
        baby grizzly is a bear cub.

*Knock, knock.*
*Who's there?*
*Alison.*
*Alison who?*
        Alison to the wolves howl at the moon.

*What does Santa say when he's finished with the eastern states?*
> Westward ho, ho, ho.

*Why did the pirate go to Texas?*
> He wanted to buy a ten-galleon hat.

*What is the wisest desert plant?*
> The sage-brush.

*Why did the cowgirl buy waterfront property?*
> Because she could 'ford the river.

*What do you call twin boys in California?*
> Son-sets in the West.

*How did the eagle get into the movies?*
    He was discovered by a talon scout.

*Why didn't the sun rise?*
    It put on its day brakes.

*What place do you avoid when you owe money?*
    Debt Valley.

*Why was Sherlock so happy in Texas?*
    He was Holmes on the range.

*What did the first Western reporters write about?*
    They covered wagons.

*What did the sausage-maker say to his son?*
        Go wurst, young man.

*What is round and well-spoken?*
        A wagon wheel.

*What kind of snake talks a lot?*
        A prattle-snake.

# Chapter Four
# Moseying to Town

*Why did the sheriff mow the grass?*
    He wanted law 'n' order.

*When can't your sneakers talk?*
    When they're hoarse shoes.

*What do you call dull horses?*
    Neigh-bores.

*Where do hypnotists go for a drink?*
    The Last Trance Saloon.

*Why was it so noisy in the cemetery?*
    Because of the tombs' tones.

A spunky stage driver named Lil
Cried out, "Get the mail through I will!"
    She drove day and night
    Through heat, hail, and blight;
I betcha she's drivin' on still.


*Why don't Texas cockroaches leave their stoves?*
    They're home on the range.


*What did Juliet say when she wanted to see a round-up?*
    "O rodeo, rodeo! Wherefore art thou, rodeo?"

*Where do heifers eat lunch?*
    At the calf-eteria.

*What do you call a rush to the post office?*
    A stamp-ede.

*What's the worst way to get mail delivered?*
    The Pony Yuk-spress.

*Knock, knock.*
*Who's there?*
*Daybreak.*
*Daybreak who?*
    Daybreak down the door to find the robber.

LAURA: I think the pioneer woman married a bad guy.
POLLY: Right, but he was caught right after the
    ceremony.
LAURA: You mean he was wedded off at the pass?

DAISY: Have you noticed that Elsie the Cow gets a lot
    of mail-order booklets?
BUTTERCUP: Yes. She wants to build a cabin.
DAISY: How is she going to build her cabin?
BUTTERCUP: With cattle logs.

*Knock, knock.*
*Who's there?*
*Guitar.*
*Guitar who?*
>Guitar luggage, we're leaving town.

*What did the wind say to the innkeeper?*
>I just blew into town.

*What's the difference between a posse and the wind?*
>One kicks up dust. The other picks up gust.

Tex: Say, Hank, I see your neckerchief is torn.
Hank: Yeah, Tex. It's a bandanna split.

*Knock, knock.*
*Who's there?*
*Alamo.*
*Alamo who?*
Alamo the grass now.

*Where do cowboys sing their final song?*
Last Chants Saloon.

*Knock, knock.*
*Who's there?*
*Saloon.*
*Saloon who?*
   Saloon, it's been good to know you.

# Chapter Five
# Ride 'em, Cowboy

JESSE: I think I'm gonna have to fire that cowboy.
RED: Why, what's he done?
JESSE: He's always trying to stirrup trouble.
RED: I thought maybe he didn't dress properly for work.
JESSE: That's true, too. He does wear a vile, vile vest.

*What's the difference between the place you tie up
your horse and a party-giving ball player?*

> One's a hitching post, the other is a
> pitching host.

*Knock, knock.*
*Who's there?*
*Stirrup.*
*Stirrup who?*

> Stirrup off your clothes and let's
> go for a swim.

*Knock, knock.*
*Who's there?*
*Dude.*
*Dude who?*
Dude drop in.

*How do cowboys see where they're going at night?*
With saddle-lights.

*What do sleepy cowgirls sing?*
Ho-hum on the range.

*What do a sharpshooter and a speedy artist have in common?*
They're both quick on the draw.

*Why couldn't the honest cowboy sleep?*
      Because of all the rustlin' going on.

*Why wasn't the cowgirl allowed to wear her neckerchief?*
      Because it was a banned-danna.

*When does a cowboy decide what boots he'll wear?*
      On the spur of the moment.

PAT: Why does that cowboy keep tripping? Are his
      boots too big?
MARTIN: No, it's that funny plant that gets in his way.
PAT: What funny plant?
MARTIN: Stumbleweed.

*What did the cowboy say to the deep-sea diver?*
      "How deep, pardner?"

*What kind of cowboy will lend you money?*
      A loan-some cowboy.

KATE: Look, the cowgirl is trying to lasso a boat.
LUCY: That's crazy. She should stick to roping steers.
KATE: She did it! She lassoed a boat!
LUCY: She must have used her lari-yacht.

*What do you call the author of a rodeo story?*
     A horse-back writer.

*What do you call a cowboy who boasts?*
     A saddle-brag.

*Why did the cowboy put his sleeping bag at the edge of a cliff?*
     He wanted to drop off to sleep.

# Chapter Six
# Gold Rush

GOLD MINER #1: I'm giving up this work.

GOLD MINER #2: Why? Yukon do it!

GOLD MINER #1: Not anymore. It's all in vein.

GOLD MINER #2: Guess you're disappointed it didn't pan out.

GOLD MINER #1: I just don't want to strain myself any longer.

GOLD MINER #2: What about all the gold that remains?

GOLD MINER #1: Oh, never mined.

*Knock, knock.*
*Who's there?*
*Nugget.*
*Nugget who?*
        Nugget off. You're bothering me.

*What tool do you bring to a gold rush?*
Take your pick.

*Why did monsters go to California?*
It was the ghoul rush.

*What is the difference between a forty-niner and a meat eater?*
One stakes a claim. The other claims a steak.

*What is a forty-niner's favorite candy?*
Gold nougats.

*What was the forty-niners' mascot?*
A mynah bird.

*What did the gold miner say when he staked out his property?*

    Be mine.


MINER FRED: Do you like your work, Ted?
MINER TED: Yup! I really dig it.


*Where did the river lay its head to sleep?*
    In the river bed.